DAILY CREATIVE

DAILY CREATIVE

THE 5-MINUTE HABIT
TO REWIRE YOUR BRAIN

BY
BLYTHE HARRIS AND MALLORY MAY

CHRONICLE BOOKS
SAN FRANCISCO

Copyright © 2026 by Blythe Harris and Mallory May.

All rights reserved. No part of this product may be reproduced in any form without written permission from the publisher.

ISBN 978-1-7972-3896-8

Manufactured in China.

Artwork by Blythe Harris and Mallory May.
Design by Blythe Harris, Mallory May, and Wynne Au-Yeung.

10 9 8 7 6 5 4 3 2

Chronicle books and gifts are available at special quantity discounts to corporations, professional associations, literacy programs, and other organizations. For details and discount information, please contact our premiums department at corporatesales@chroniclebooks.com or at 1-800-759-0190.

Chronicle Books LLC
680 Second Street
San Francisco, California 94107
www.chroniclebooks.com

CONTENTS

Unlock Your Innate Creativity   **8**

PART I: CLEARING   17
Create Space for Inspiration to Flow

PART II: PLAY   37
Warm Up and Let Go of Perfectionism

PART III: NOTICING   69
Open Your Senses

PART IV: CONSTRAINTS   99
Discover the Power of Limitations to Inspire Creativity

PART V: POINT OF VIEW   147
Find Your Creative Voice

PART VI: INTEGRATION   165
Pull It All Together

UNLOCK YOUR INNATE CREATIVITY

Whether you think of yourself as creative or not,

YOU BELONG HERE.

Everyone has creativity within them, an inner *aliveness*—it's the unique way that you synthesize and express your experience of the world around you. Along your journey, your connection with your creativity may have wavered. Maybe a teacher frowned at your drawing or you got a mediocre grade on a short story and you started telling yourself you were "not creative." We are here to change that narrative.

CREATIVITY IS INNATE

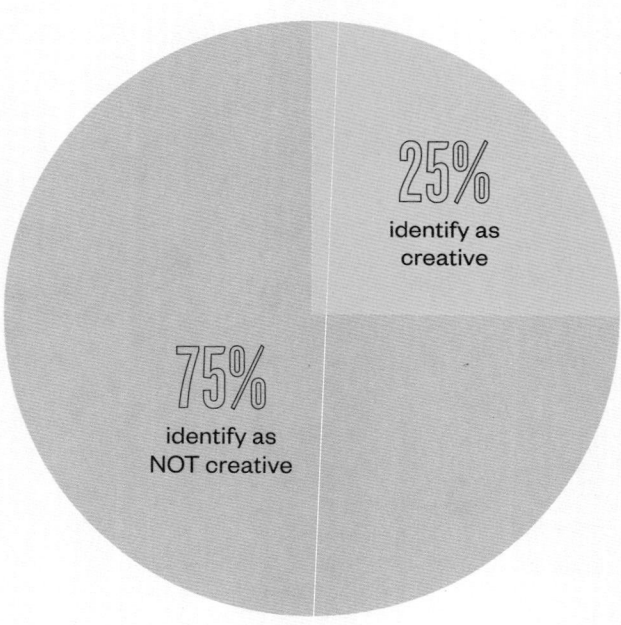

Did you know that 75 percent of people identify as "NOT creative"? However, this is not true...

Creativity is innate but requires nourishment and practice, just like our muscles require exercise. Think of this journal as a daily mini workout for your creative brain, filled with our favorite bite-size prompts to help you spark inspiration and tap into your unique perspective. No previous skills required!

Most importantly, this journal is about having fun. There's no *right* or *wrong* way to do these exercises. At DailyCreative, we are proudly anti-perfectionist. Come as you are. Let your heart lead. Regardless of what ends up on the page, you've begun your day by activating your innate creativity—paving the way for a more open, flexible, and innovative mind.

— **BLYTHE & MALLORY**

EVERYONE IS CREATIVE! CREATIVITY IS INNATE— IT JUST NEEDS NOURISHMENT.

THE SCIENCE IS CLEAR: CREATIVITY ISN'T FIXED—IT'S FLEXIBLE. WITH CONSISTENT PRACTICE, IT GROWS STRONGER OVER TIME.

THE BENEFITS OF CREATIVITY

Let's face it: Modern life has made our brains a little lazy. With so much automated and optimized for comfort, we rarely stretch beyond routine. But when we stop challenging our brains, they lose some of their flexibility and vitality—exactly what we need to adapt in a world of rapid change.

Here's the good news: Engaging in new creative activities, even for just a few minutes a day, stimulates the brain's reward system, boosts dopamine, and promotes neuroplasticity—the brain's ability to adapt and form new connections. In other words, creativity doesn't just feel good—it actively strengthens and reshapes your brain.

CREATIVITY...

Expands brain plasticity

Improves mental health

Increases happiness

Alleviates stress and anxiety

Sharpens problem-solving skills

Exercises memory and recall

Fights dementia

Expands your perspective

Celebrates diversity

Reduces bias

Leads to self-discovery

Fuels innovative thinking

PART I

CLEARING

CREATE SPACE FOR INSPIRATION TO FLOW

Our minds are like overgrown gardens—beautiful but often tangled with weeds. The endless doomscroll, the breaking news, the to-do lists that never seem to shrink: All of it piles up, leaving us feeling stuck, sluggish, and disconnected from ourselves.

It's time to clear the clutter. To reset. To make space for fresh ideas, revived energy, and inspiration to flow freely.

Let's begin.

TWENTY WORDS

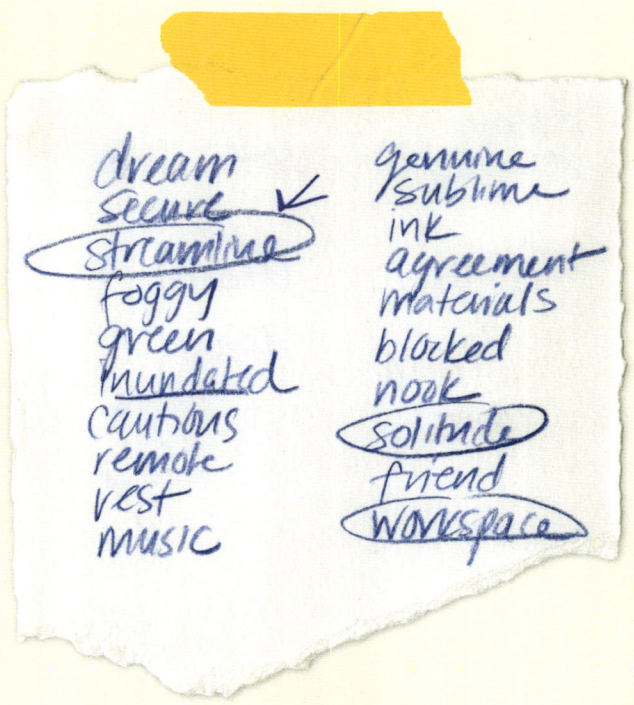

BENEFITS
Increases Neuroplasticity / Develops Self-Awareness
Reduces Stress / Fuels Imagination

Take a deep breath and then quickly write down the first twenty words that come to mind. Let the words spill out without overthinking or self-editing. Clearing your mind of clutter will help you access a flow state that will activate your creative brain. When you've finished, look through your list and circle any words that particularly resonate with you.

BILATERAL DOODLING

BENEFITS
Relieves Stress / Releases Emotions
Enhances Focus / Promotes Mental Clarity

Doodle with both hands at the same time without lifting your pen or pencil. Experiment with different speeds, pressures, and rhythms. Don't worry about what it looks like; just focus on the process.

BILATERAL DOODLING
Part II

Now try completely different motions with each hand.

BILATERAL DOODLING
Part III

Now try closing your eyes while you doodle.

DAYDREAMING

BENEFITS
Strengthens Memory and Recall / Creates New Neural Pathways
Enhances Emotional Processing

Close your eyes and try to remember sounds from your past (examples: ice cream truck, the school bell, grandfather's voice). Our ears process information in a more abstract way than our eyes. Certain sounds can trigger episodic memories, which are memories linked to a strong emotional response. Daydreaming about memories associated with sounds helps us integrate the past and present and initiate a state of mindfulness.

What sounds can you remember from growing up?

What sounds evoke strong emotions?

Write down one powerful memory that is associated with sound.

INTUITION

Intuition is that quiet, knowing voice inside you—the one that understands before you do and that guides you without explanation. It's the bridge between experience and insight, between the subconscious and sudden flashes of inspiration. When you trust it, creativity flows more freely.

Intuition helps you bypass overthinking and perfectionism, allowing you to make unexpected connections and tap into ideas that logic alone might miss. It fuels originality, problem-solving, and self-expression, opening doors to new ways of thinking.

Want to strengthen your intuition? Start by listening to even the softest inner nudges—the fleeting urge to pick up a book, take a different route home, or explore an idea that sparks curiosity. The more you follow these quiet instincts, the louder and clearer they become.

INTUITIVE WRITING

BENEFITS

Relieves Stress / Releases Emotions / Enhances Focus and Mental Clarity
Builds Dexterity / Promotes Relaxation and Mind Wandering

Start writing in one continuous line without planning or using structured letters or language. Let the hand lead and the mind rest. Focus on the process, not the result. Allow the expressive movements to be spontaneous, unplanned, and driven by intuition, instinct, and rhythm. The repetition and continuity of making these lines promote a calming effect, quiet distractions, and help clear the mind.

WORD ASSOCIATION

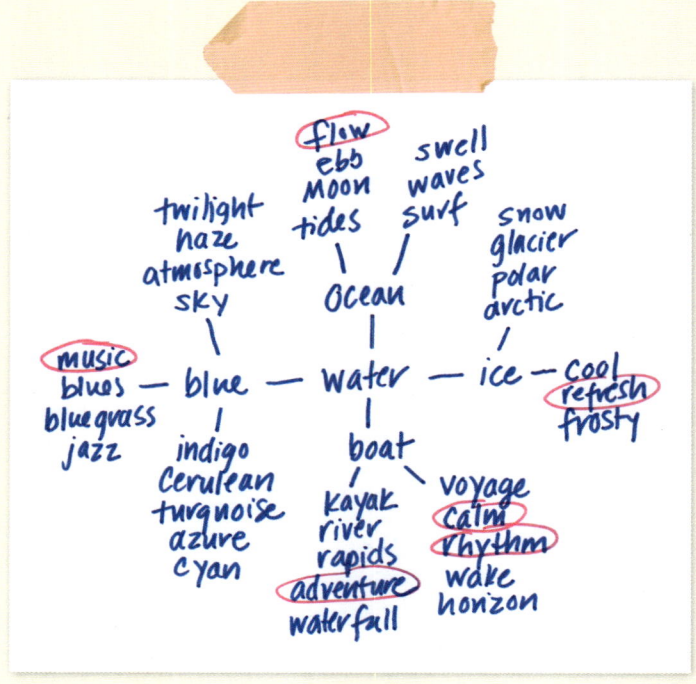

BENEFITS

Boosts Lateral Thinking / Enhances Idea Generation
Supports Cognitive Flexibility

Write a word, then connect it to another four words that come to mind. Keep going and try to get to five- to ten-word association chains. Notice if any themes or patterns emerge.

PART II

WARM UP AND LET GO OF PERFECTIONISM

The fun starts here. Say goodbye to creativity killers like perfectionism and overthinking, and hello to presence and joy. When you stop focusing on *results*, your brain rewards you with a rush of dopamine that enhances your inner play and leads to creative flow.

THREE DOTS

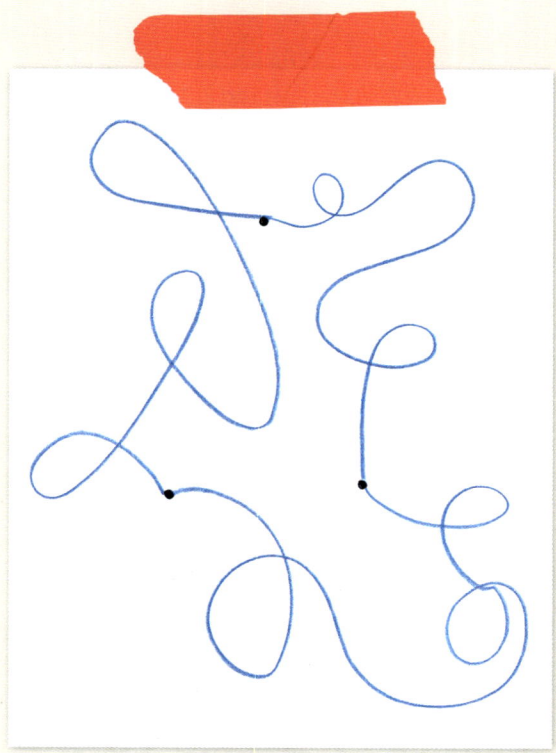

BENEFITS
Boosts Focus / Reduces Perfectionism

Connect each set of three dots without picking up your pen or pencil. Make as many different shapes as possible, using varying line pathways. How many different possibilities can you create?

FOUR DOTS
Straight and Curvy Lines

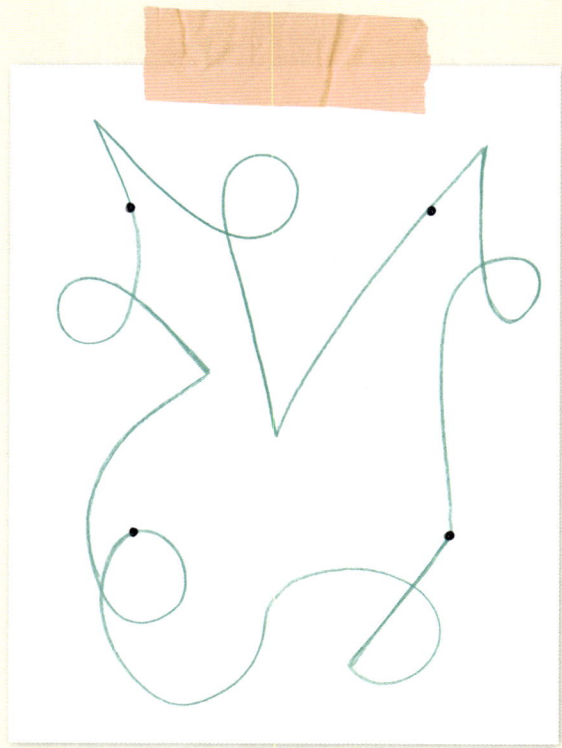

BENEFITS
Boosts Focus / Reduces Perfectionism
Promotes Mindfulness / Stimulates Divergent Thinking

Connect each of the four sets of dots without picking up your pen or pencil. Make as many different shapes as possible, using varying line pathways. Use both straight *and* curvy lines.

FIVE DOTS
Straight Lines Only

BENEFITS
Boosts Focus / Reduces Perfectionism
Promotes Mindfulness / Stimulates Divergent Thinking

Connect each of the five sets of dots without picking up your pen or pencil. Make as many different shapes as possible, using varying line pathways. Use straight lines only.

COLOR NAMING

BENEFITS

Activates Memory / Stimulates Innovative Thinking

Tune in to your intuition and create names for each color below. Consider what each shade reminds you of and activate your memory. Avoid obvious color names and associations, and challenge yourself to connect with your personal or sensory experience of the color.

COLOR CLOUDS

BENEFITS
Increases Intuition / Heightens Perceptual Awareness
Boosts Creative Thinking

Using colored pencils, markers, or crayons, create a "cloud" with any combination of colors. This is a playful, low-pressure way to explore color and experiment freely. Try it several times with different colors and shapes, letting your intuition guide you. As you experiment, notice which colors are most pleasing and which surprise you the most.

LINE AND RHYTHM

BENEFITS

Increases Sensory Perception / Heightens Intuition
Builds New Neural Connections

Pick two or three different songs and draw a line while listening to each one. Respond intuitively to the rhythm without overthinking. Music is a powerful sensory input that stimulates every region of the brain. Each sound has a unique vibration and rhythm that can be abstracted into visual expression, and drawing to music is a great way to engage in sensory integration, an important skill for creative problem-solving.

INTUITIVE COLOR

BENEFITS
Enhances Symbolic Thinking / Enhances Intuition
Promotes Sensory Integration

Create a color palette for your favorite film or novel (our example was inspired by Wes Anderson films). Reflect on memorable scenes and the colors you intuitively associate with the experience. Remember, it does not have to be literal, but it should be fun.

LINE AND CONTOUR

BENEFITS

Boosts Mindfulness and Relaxation / Stimulates Visual Processing and Spatial Awareness / Exercises Motor Skills and Coordination

Starting anywhere in the workspace, draw a wavy line across the page. Following the contour of your line, draw subsequent lines, loosely tracing the outline of the previous line like the lines on a topographic map. Keep going to the edges of the page in each direction. Try varying the thickness of lines and embrace imperfections—they yield a more interesting result!

THE SPIRAL

Spirals are a universal structure in nature, present in seashells, galaxies, and even our own human DNA. The spiral motif has appeared in art throughout history, from ancient art and architecture and illuminated manuscripts to the paintings and sculptures of more contemporary artists like Robert Smythson, Louise Bourgeois, and Hilma af Klint. A symbol of growth, transformation, and connection to the divine, the spiral captivates and invites contemplation.

Drawing spirals is a form of *focused doodling* that is both meditative and mesmerizing. Louise Bourgeois noted in her essay "Spiral" that drawing a spiral from the inside out creates an experience of "giving, and giving up control; of trust [and] positive energy" while drawing a spiral from the outside in feels like a "tightening, a retreating, a compacting to the point of disappearance."

SPIRALS

Outside-In Spiral

Start here
•

BENEFITS
Reduces Stress / Boosts Focus and Mindfulness / Promotes Mind Wandering

Draw two spirals, one starting on the outside edge of the workspace and one starting in the center. Pay attention to the sensation of drawing each spiral.

SINGLE LINE DRAWING

BENEFITS

Helps Access a State of Play / Reduces Perfectionism
Promotes Mindfulness / Sharpens Problem-Solving Skills

Find an object in your space and focus on it. Draw it using a single, unbroken line—no lifting your pen, no second-guessing. Instead of outlining, let your line wander, crossing through the form where it feels right. Imagine you're an ant crawling over its surface, tracing every curve and edge. Let go of perfection. This exercise is about movement, not precision—loosening your grip, quieting your mind, and slipping into a creative flow.

NONDOMINANT HAND

BENEFITS

Activates New Neural Pathways / Reduces Perfectionism
Encourages Adaptability / Improves Dexterity

Using your nondominant hand, sketch something in your line of sight or free doodle. Embrace the freedom from perfectionism and let go of the control you are used to with your dominant hand. Enjoy the fun of drawing like a child again and relish a sense of play.

LINE AND SHAPE

BENEFITS
Enhances Cognitive Flexibility / Reduces Stress / Sparks Imagination

Let your pen roam freely across the page, filling the space with a wild, looping scribble. No plan, no hesitation—just movement. As the lines overlap, notice the shapes that appear. Color in some of the shapes and observe how they are activated by the colors you choose.

LINE AND PERSPECTIVE

BENEFITS
Enhances Visual-Spatial Skills / Improves Dexterity
Expands Your Perspective

Draw a series of lines, starting at the bottom of the page, that bend at a wide angle. The lines should gradually decrease in size and thickness as you move up the page. Decrease the space between each line as you move up the page. Notice the illusion this creates and the sense of perspective—the lines appear to move back in space.

PART III

NOTICING

OPEN YOUR SENSES

Do you ever feel as if you are moving through life on autopilot? In order to navigate the repetitive routines of daily life, our minds conserve energy by taking shortcuts, dulling our sense of curiosity and aliveness. Noticing is the antidote—a simple, powerful practice that pulls us back into the present, reawakens our curiosity, and opens the door to creativity. The more we pay attention, the more beauty we find. Bonus: Noticing cultivates gratitude, turning even the smallest details into sources of joy.

SOUND

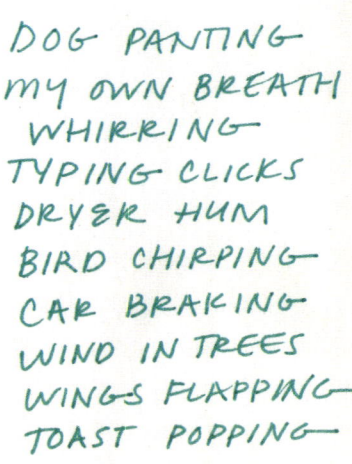

DOG PANTING
MY OWN BREATH
WHIRRING
TYPING CLICKS
DRYER HUM
BIRD CHIRPING
CAR BRAKING
WIND IN TREES
WINGS FLAPPING
TOAST POPPING

BENEFITS

Strengthens Attention and Concentration / Reduces Stress
Builds Neural Pathways / Heightens Imagination

Close your eyes and take a moment to listen to the sounds around you. What is the farthest sound you can hear? What is the closest sound you can hear? Pay attention to the qualities of each sound and where you feel it in your body. List five distinct sounds that you can hear, starting from the closest and ending with the farthest.

TOUCH

BENEFITS

Improves Attention to Detail / Increases Sensory Perception
Heightens Imagination

Choose a three-dimensional object to examine closely through touch. Closing your eyes, trace the object with your hands, noticing the form, texture, shape, and weight. Write down your observations of the object. What surprised you? What adjectives would you use to describe the object? What would you have missed if you had not touched it?

TEXTURE

BENEFITS
Sharpens Observational Skills / Increases a Sense of Presence
Integrates the Senses of Sight and Touch

Select two or three everyday objects of varying sizes and textures. Close your eyes and run your fingers over the surfaces, closely observing each texture. Create a series of lines that convey each texture and the feeling of the form that you have discovered. Pay careful attention to the slightest undulations and quirks in your lines; they will reflect what is interesting and unique.

POSITIVE AND NEGATIVE SPACE

BENEFITS
Encourages Attention and Focus / Reduces Stress
Builds Neural Pathways / Heightens Imagination

Draw two shapes that overlap the center line in the workspace. Pick a color and shade the *inside* of the shapes on the left-hand side and the empty space, or "negative space," around the shapes on the right-hand side. Fill in the remaining spaces with a second color. Notice what patterns emerge, what new shapes are created, and the satisfying feeling of completing it.

NOTICING COLOR

BENEFITS
Stimulates Visual Processing / Increases Focus and Mindfulness
Increases Visual Memory

Choose any color and spend the next five minutes observing every instance of it in your surroundings. You can stay in place or move around. How many variations do you notice? Pay attention to subtle shifts in your chosen color. Record your favorites below.

COLOR COMBINATIONS

BENEFITS

Stimulates Visual Processing / Increases Focus
Promotes Mindfulness / Increases Visual Memory

Take a five-minute walk to discover interesting color combinations that catch your eye. Find inspiration in everything around you, from packaging and food to clothing, nature, and even unexpected places like street signs. Which combinations interest you the most? Take note of your favorites and re-create them below.

COLOR

Color shapes the way we see the world—it sparks emotion, sets a mood, and fuels creativity in ways we don't always realize. As artist Wassily Kandinsky said in *Concerning the Spiritual in Art*, "Color is a power that directly influences the soul." Discovering what colors and combinations resonate for you can be an exciting part of the creative process.

Color is created when light hits an object and is reflected to our eye. We each perceive color in our own unique way, and across all cultures, colors carry distinct meanings and associations.

The color wheel helps us understand elements of color, such as hue, value, and saturation, as well as how colors interact with each other, giving us a framework for using color with intention.

Learning to see and understand color more deeply won't just enhance your creativity—it will change the way you experience the world.

Warm colors

Cool colors

Hue
The pure color

Value
The degree of lightness
or darkness of a color

Saturation
The vividness or
purity of a color

COLOR HARMONY

Have you ever wondered why certain colors work well together, while others clash or are visually unappealing? Understanding color harmony is a simple starting point to help you combine colors effectively.

Artists and designers in the fashion, interior design, and advertising worlds all work with color harmony to create balance, contrast, and rich complexity through color. While all color interpretation is subjective, here are some basic guidelines on how certain harmonic combinations can evoke emotion.

Monochromatic and **analogous** color combinations can create a feeling of calm. Think of the gradient of a sunset, or the calm of a monochromatic room.

Complementary colors have more friction and contrast, creating a sense of aliveness and energy.

Triadic color palettes are balanced and complex, especially when varying in saturation and value.

Monochromatic
A single color

Analogous
2–4 colors next to each other on the color wheel

Complementary
Colors opposite each other on the color wheel

Triadic
Any three colors spaced evenly on the color wheel

COMPLEMENTARY

BENEFITS

Builds Visual Sensitivity / Stimulates New Neural Connections
Encourages Risk-Taking

Experiment with color by creating a series of complementary color schemes (complementary colors are colors opposite from each other on the color wheel). Remember to play around with value and saturation to make more unexpected combinations. Make note of what you think works best for the most pleasing combinations.

ANALOGOUS

BENEFITS

Enhances Color Sensitivity / Strengthens Visual Perception
Refines Visual Harmony Skills

Fill in each section with an analogous color scheme (analogous colors are the two to four colors next to each other on the color wheel). Play around with variations and placement, and continue to experiment with varying values and saturations, using light, dark, and muted shades of your colors. Make note of what you think works best for the most pleasing combinations.

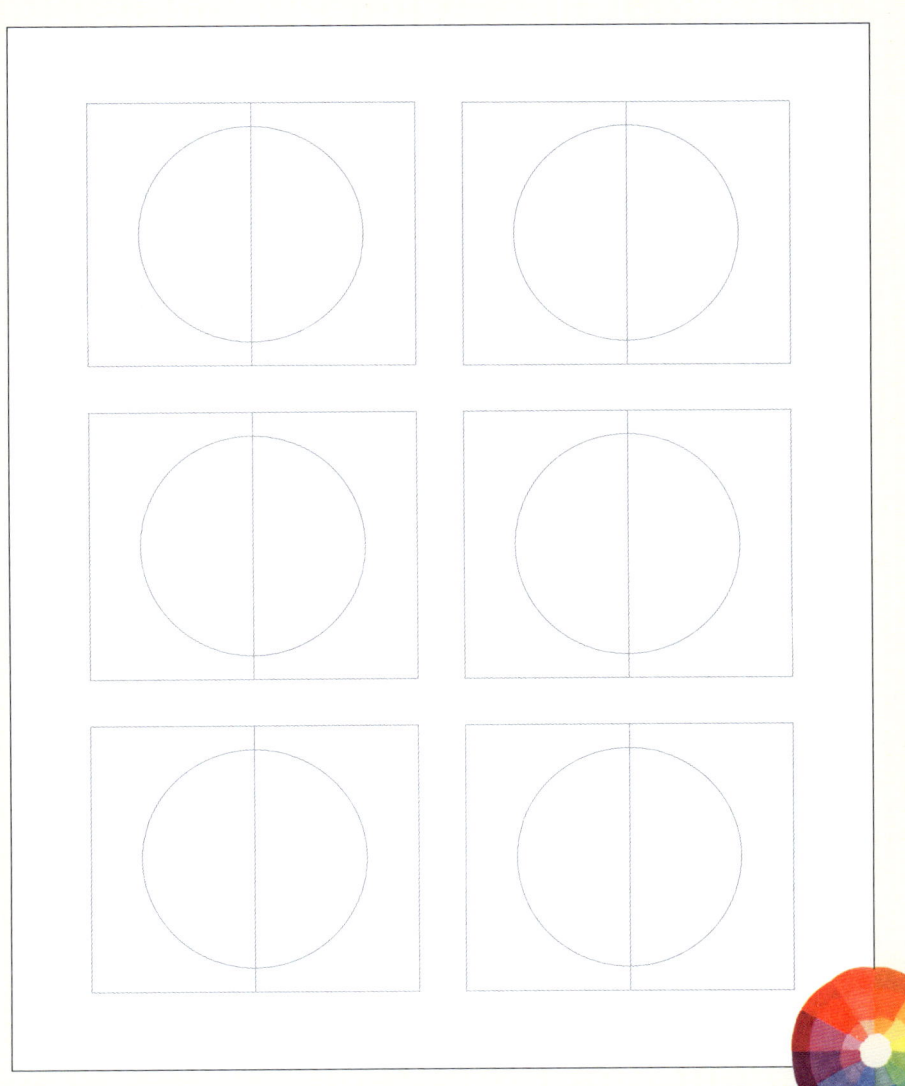

TRIADIC

BENEFITS

Promotes Exploration / Engages the Visual Cortex
Encourages Aesthetic Intuition / Supports Design Thinking

Choose three triadic color schemes (triadic colors are any three colors spaced evenly on the color wheel) and experiment by creating blocks of your chosen colors in the spaces below. Remember, you can use light, dark, or muted shades of your colors. Make note of what you think works best for the most pleasing combinations.

STRIPES

BENEFITS

Engages the Visual Cortex / Encourages Aesthetic Intuition
Refines Aesthetic Judgment / Promotes Creative Exploration

Creating striped patterns is a fun way to play around with your favorite color combinations. Draw parallel lines of varying colors and widths in the spaces below. When you start to create a stripe, you will notice that certain combinations slow the eye down, while others speed it up. In other words, you can create your own *rhythm* through your color choices. Explore hue, value, saturation, and color harmony to find which types of combinations appeal to you most.

UGLY COLOR SCHEME

BENEFITS
Reduces Bias / Strengthens Mental Flexibility
Increases Awareness / Refines Visual Sensitivity

Create an ugly color scheme. This might be harder than you think! Try not to choose only colors you dislike. Use your intuition to select colors that you don't think work well together. Remember, you can use both bright and muted colors. Were you successful?

PART IV
CONSTRAINTS

DISCOVER THE POWER OF LIMITATIONS TO INSPIRE CREATIVITY

Rules and boundaries aren't barriers; they are tools. They strip away the overthinking, the second-guessing, and the endless "Where do I even start?" Instead, they give you a place to begin—an open door instead of a blank page. The following constraints are designed to help remove overwhelm and access a state of creative flow.

It turns out *limitations* can be *liberating*.

DOTS AND LINES

BENEFITS

Encourages Mind Wandering / Improves Pattern Recognition Skills
Promotes Idea Generation / Builds Spatial Awareness

Make an even number of dots randomly distributed over the workspace. We recommend at least twenty dots. Connect all the points with straight lines. This exercise is based on Sol LeWitt's conceptual approach to making art, shifting focus from outcome-based to process-based creativity.

PATTERN

BENEFITS

Promotes Idea Generation / Fosters Self-Expression / Improves Focus
Encourages Mindfulness / Stimulates Visual-Spatial Skills

Using a pencil or pen, create a pattern using a letter (try your first initial). Doodle with that letter and experiment with shape, orientation, and scale. You can try different line weights, incorporate block or cursive styles, or add texture. Notice how the shapes transform when you flip them around and the forms that emerge.

SCALE

BENEFITS
Shifts Perspective / Sharpens Attention to Detail
Strengthens Working Memory / Promotes Cognitive Flexibility

Using your pattern from the previous exercise as a starting point, play with scale by zooming in on a section and drawing it larger, or by scaling out, making the pattern smaller with more repetition. Shifting scale by zooming in or out gives you a different perspective, showing how forms interact and emphasizing overall structure and relationships. Practicing at different scales is a great way to explore those relationships and can lead to discovery.

DIVIDING A RECTANGLE

BENEFITS
Encourages Lateral Thinking / Fosters Problem-Solving
Increases Neuroplasticity / Promotes Playfulness and Idea Generation

Divide each of the rectangles below with a different curved line and color in the resulting shapes. This exercise is inspired by the sketchbooks of one of our favorite artists, Ellsworth Kelly, who devoted page after page to discovering how many ways a curve could *inhabit* a rectangle. His minimalist approach is a fun way to explore color and composition.

FOUND POETRY

WALK-ABOUT

...most extraordinary...my own...a dream...our own...

125

BENEFITS

Leads to Self-Discovery / Sharpens Problem-Solving Skills
Promotes Adaptability and Divergent Thinking

Using the provided text as a starting point, find the "poem" within by identifying the words or phrases that stand out for you, and cross out the rest with a marker.

The ocean stretched endlessly before him, a living tapestry of blues and greens fringed by the golden light of dawn. Grey's toes trailed in the cool water, the gentle rise and fall of the swell beneath him a familiar, comforting rhythm. He waited, eyes scanning the horizon for the next wave, but there was no impatience in his heart—only a deep, abiding sense of wonder.

He had chased waves across the world: the thundering barrels of Indonesia, the icy perfection of Norway's arctic shores, the sun-soaked breaks of Australia, and the wild, untamed coasts of South America. Each journey had been an escape, a passage forward, a way to outrun the darkness that sometimes crept in during the quiet moments. He'd filled his years with motion, with the extraordinary joy of discovery, the resonance of new languages, new friends, new loves.

Yet as he sat in the gentle embrace of his home break, the familiar cliffs rising behind him and the scent of salt and wildflowers drifting from the shore, he felt something shift. The river of his life, once flowing so swiftly, seemed too slow in this place he'd always called a temporary stop.

CHANCE DOODLE

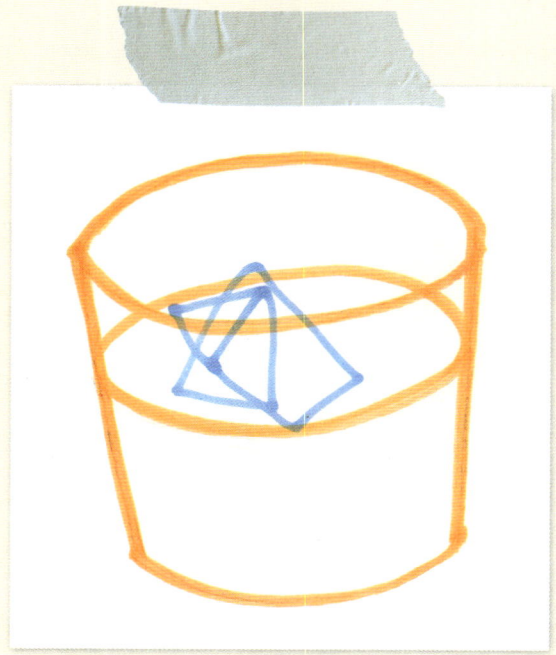

BENEFITS

Reduces Perfectionism / Stimulates Pattern Recognition and Emergent Thinking
Encourages a Perspective Shift / Strengthens Cognitive Flexibility

Close your eyes and make a random doodle in the workspace. When completed, open your eyes and use the doodle as a starting point to create a drawing. An exercise in chance, this process stimulates the brain in a unique way by introducing unpredictability and requiring reinterpretation and creative thinking.

BLIND CONTOUR

BENEFITS
Reduces Perfectionism / Encourages Adaptability
Heightens Perception

Choose an object in your sight line. Without looking at your paper, keep your eyes fixed on the subject and slowly trace its edges and details while moving your pencil in sync. Do not lift your pencil or peek at the page—trust your hand to follow what your eyes see. The goal is not accuracy but deep observation. Embrace imperfection and strengthen your ability to truly see, rather than draw from memory or habit.

SIX-WORD STORY

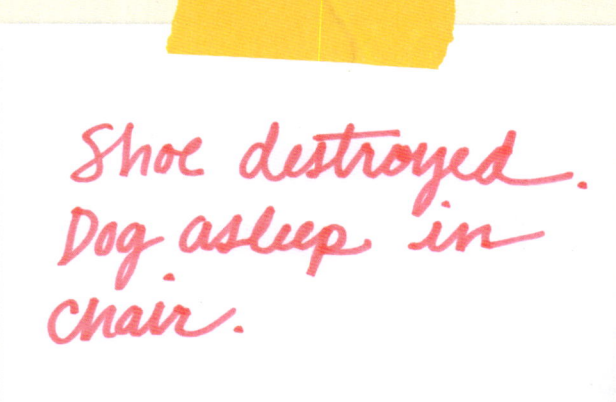

BENEFITS
Improves Cognitive Efficiency / Sharpens Communication Skills
Encourages Adaptability

Write a complete story in just six words. Attempt to convey as much information as possible with efficiency. Include as much action and emotion in these six words as possible. Tip: Pick an emotion and make sure the story conveys it.

THE GRID

Our brains thrive on structured exploration to generate ideas. The grid helps organize visual elements, creating balance, rhythm, and harmony. The *real* magic happens when we use its framework for exploration. Our brains thrive on structured exploration to generate ideas. The grid naturally eliminates the pressure of perfectionism, shifting your focus to playfulness and freedom of expression. It provides a perfect structure with infinite possibilities that encourages learning and stimulates new connections.

THREE REASONS WE LOVE USING THE GRID

Innovation: Grids provide a framework that naturally encourages experimentation, leading to discovery!

Process over perfection: Using a grid shifts the focus to process, iteration, and change by removing the pressure of perfection.

Natural organization: The grid helps organize visual elements, making it easy to experiment with balance, rhythm, and harmony.

WHY ARTISTS USE THE GRID

Organization: The grid helps organize the visual elements of a piece, creating balance, rhythm, and harmony (Josef Albers, Piet Mondrian, Chuck Close).

Creative constraints and innovation: Grids provide a framework that encourages experimentation within boundaries, challenging artists to innovate within a structured format (Sol LeWitt, Gerhard Richter, Yayoi Kusama).

Accuracy: Grids allow artists to translate and scale images accurately, maintaining proportion and alignment when working on larger or more detailed compositions (Leonardo da Vinci, Albrecht Dürer).

Meditation: The structured, repetitive process of drawing or painting on a grid can be done to calm the mind (Agnes Martin, Vija Celmins, Emma Kunz).

GRID

BENEFITS

Activates Problem-Solving Skills / Enhances Spatial Awareness
Improves Fine Motor Coordination / Encourages Meditation

Using the grid as a starting point and a guide, create a design with a pencil or marker. There are no limitations beyond the grid, so jump in and see what shapes and patterns emerge.

REACTIVE GRID

BENEFITS

Enhances Fine Motor Skills / Refines Spatial Reasoning
Increases Focus / Sharpens Visual Processing

Draw two to four shapes in the workspace, and then make a series of vertical lines from the top of the page to the bottom, tracing around the shapes. Next, draw horizontal lines across the page, again moving around the shapes to create an undulating grid pattern. Try not to get caught up in perfectionism; take liberties instead, as this can sometimes lead to an even more interesting outcome.

DIRECTIONAL LINES

BENEFITS
Promotes Spatial Awareness / Engages Visual Processing
Activates Visual and Conceptual Thinking / Encourages Creative Adaptability

Drawing freehand, create a grid in the workspace. It's OK to have more vertical lines than horizontal. Embrace imperfection! No rulers are allowed, and it's fine if the individual boxes are of different widths or sizes. When your grid is complete, fill in each square with a horizontal, vertical, or diagonal line. The diagonal lines should extend from corner to corner in an upward or downward direction. This exercise is inspired by Sol LeWitt's conceptual wall drawings.

PRINCIPLES OF DESIGN

The principles of design are used by designers as guidelines to help create visually balanced, engaging, and effective compositions. Understanding these principles and exploring them is a great way to activate your creativity and make new discoveries.

Balance: Establishes harmony through equally distributed visual weight

Repetition: Creates patterns using repeating elements

Emphasis: Directs attention to the most important elements

Movement: Guides the viewer's eye through the design

Variety: Introduces diversity in elements

White space: Enhances visual impact through intentional empty spaces around design elements (also known as *negative space*)

BALANCE

REPETITION

EMPHASIS

MOVEMENT

VARIETY

WHITE SPACE

BALANCE

BENEFITS

Activates a Flow State / Promotes Logical Reasoning
Stimulates Innovative Thinking

Create a design in the grid by adding shapes to each box while paying attention to *balance*. Try to add equal visual weight to each section of the grid. One easy way to achieve balance is through *symmetry*, by mirroring the same shapes and colors on each side of the grid.

REPETITION

BENEFITS

Enhances Pattern Recognition and Predictive Processing
Strengthens Working Memory / Engages Both Logical and Creative Thinking
Boosts Focus and Induces a Flow State

Create a design in the grid with *repetition* by using the same shapes or colors. Repetition tends to be very soothing to the eye and is an easy way to create a compelling composition.

EMPHASIS

BENEFITS

Boosts Selective Attention and Focus / Engages Hierarchical Thinking
Engages Abstract Reasoning

Create *emphasis* in the grid by using one element that is a different color, shape, or both. Notice how your eye is immediately drawn to the differentiated element. Using emphasis commands attention to one area.

MOVEMENT

BENEFITS
Boosts Innovative Thinking / Engages Problem-Solving Skills
Engages Abstract Reasoning

Create a design in the grid by adding shapes that suggest *movement*. Unlike emphasis, where you were attempting to hold the viewer's eye in one place, movement is about guiding the viewer on a journey through your composition. Think about the most pleasing path for the eye, using different shapes or colors.

VARIETY

BENEFITS

Strengthens Creative Confidence / Engages Problem-Solving Skills
Activates Visual and Spatial Intelligence / Engages Divergent and Convergent Thinking

Using what you have discovered while exploring the design principles, create a design in the grid with *variety*. Incorporate your favorite elements using varying shapes and colors. Take the opportunity to freestyle and let go of the rules that do not resonate with you.

WHITE SPACE

BENEFITS
Engages Visual-Spatial Skills / Induces a Flow State / Stimulates Pattern Recognition
Builds Working Memory and Problem-Solving Skills

Draw a shape in each box. Pay attention to the white space and the shapes that are created in that part of your grid as you go. Rotate the orientation of your shapes with the goal of creating interesting shapes in that empty space. When you are done, notice what shapes have emerged and how they work together in the overall composition.

REVERSE WORD ASSOCIATION

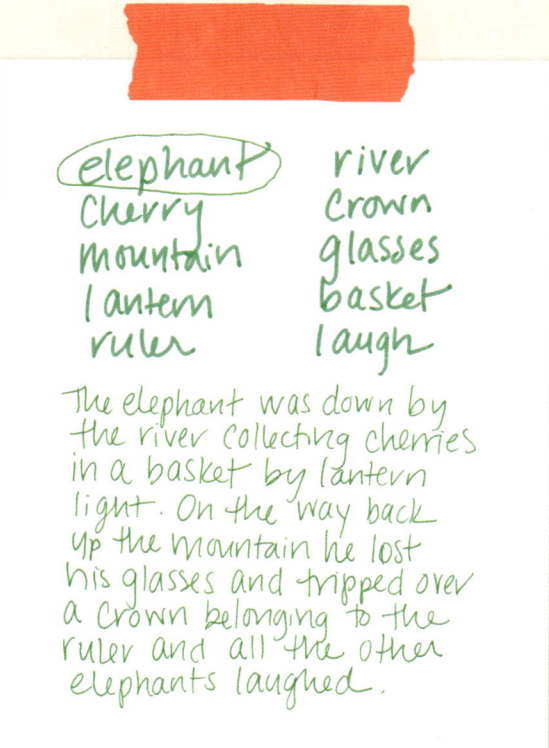

BENEFITS

Boosts Cognitive Flexibility / Stimulates Lateral and Associative Thinking
Reduces Overthinking / Builds Mental Agility and Adaptability

Choose a single word and write nine words that are *not* related to it. Once you have completed the list, find a creative way to connect your words into a brief story.

CREATE YOUR OWN RULES

BENEFITS

Encourages Divergent Thinking / Sparks Innovation
Boosts Cognitive Flexibility

Now that you've experienced how constraints or limitations can spark creativity, try making your own creative rule. For example, draw using only circles or write a short poem without the letter e. Notice how these limitations stretch you, creating a fun challenge that promotes innovative thinking.

PART V

POINT OF VIEW

FIND YOUR CREATIVE VOICE

Everyone has their own creative "fingerprint."

No one sees the world quite like you do. Your creative fingerprint is made up of the marks you make, the colors you're drawn to, and the shapes, ideas, and rhythms that feel like home. The more you explore them, the more you refine your unique style—your *point of view*.

When you embrace your creative identity, you invite more joy, freedom, and self-expression into your life, on your *own* terms. For what it's worth, that's a very good thing.

MARK MAKING

BENEFITS

Sparks Innovation / Promotes Lateral Thinking
Develops Your Unique Visual Language / Reduces Perfectionism

Let's start building your creative tool kit. Using a single pen or pencil, see how many different marks you can make in the workspace below. Experiment with thick and thin lines, dots, waves, and scribbles. Try cross-hatching. Challenge yourself to get out of your comfort zone! Think of the marks you make as your unique *visual language* that you develop over time.

MARK MAKING WITH COLOR

BENEFITS

Sparks Innovation / Promotes Divergent Thinking
Develops Your Unique Visual Language

Try introducing some of your favorite colors into your marks, noticing how it changes them and makes them more interesting or exciting. Have fun playing with the widths and styles of your marks and pay attention to where your eyes are drawn once you add color.

MARK MAKING WITH COLLAGE

BENEFITS

Encourages Risk-Taking / Fosters a Growth Mindset
Strengthens Problem-Solving Skills / Develops Your Unique Visual Language

On a loose piece of scrap paper, re-create your favorite marks and color combinations from the previous pages. Then, tear the paper into pieces and experiment with arranging them into a collage. Shift the fragments around, exploring different compositions until you find one that feels visually compelling. Note how the variation in marks and colors makes the composition more interesting and dynamic when you overlap and combine them. When you finish, glue or tape your collage onto the workspace below.

WRITE YOUR STORY

Jersey Girl
Head in the Clouds
California Bound
Sleeping Under the Stars
Encounter with a Truck
An American in Paris
And then There were Four

BENEFITS

Engages Memory Retrieval / Encourages Cognitive Organization
Strengthens Narrative Thinking and Pattern Recognition

Write a chapter title in the workspace for each major phase of your life. A key step to unlocking your creativity is self-awareness and discovery. Mining your memory and excavating your past is a great way to remember parts of your story that you might have forgotten along the way. Try using humor and have fun with it.

PERSONAL COLOR PALETTE

BENEFITS
Engages Symbolic Thinking / Strengthens Intuition
Promotes Sensory Integration

Hopefully, by now, you have a better sense of the colors you are intuitively drawn to, as well as an understanding of how colors interact with each other. Create a personal color palette in the workspace that combines all your favorite hues and combinations.

MY PLAID

BENEFITS

Engages Fine Motor Skills / Encourages a Meditative State
Increases Focus / Sharpens Visual Processing

Using your intuitive response to color and what you have discovered so far, create your own individual plaid in the workspace. Create a series of repeating horizontal and vertical lines in varying colors and widths. *Fun fact:* A tartan or plaid is a textile traditionally used in Scotland to signify family or clan.

ABSTRACT SELF-PORTRAIT

BENEFITS
Stimulates Memory Retrieval / Promotes Cognitive Organization
Strengthens Narrative Thinking

Create an abstract self-portrait in the workspace. Combine images, words, numbers, symbols, a quote, or anything else that represents you. Use any marks, lines, or colors from the previous exercises that resonated with you. Here are a few additional prompts for inspiration:

If you were a color combination, what would it be?
If you got a tattoo, what would it be?
Is there one item that best represents your style?
If you had to pick a song lyric, what would it be?
If you were a place, where would that be?

PART VI

INTEGRATION

PULL IT ALL TOGETHER

Congratulations on making it this far on your creative journey.

You have...

> *Let go of perfectionism and leaned into a sense of play.*
>
> *Learned to notice the world around you with all five senses, sparking your curiosity and collecting threads of inspiration.*
>
> *Used constraints to challenge your perspective and open your horizons.*
>
> *Explored your unique creative fingerprint, or what we like to call your point of view.*

Now it's time to make creativity a habit...

MY FAVORITES

TWENTY WORDS
(COLOR CLOUDS)
NOTICING COLOR
REACTIVE GRID
FOUND POETRY

Reflect on which exercises sparked your curiosity and joy. Write a list of your five favorites, then circle the one that you would like to try every day for one week as a daily creative practice.

At the end of each week, look back on your work and notice any themes or patterns that emerge. For example, if you selected "Twenty Words," are there certain words that keep popping up or themes that unfold over time? As you start to notice patterns, you will gain a deeper understanding of your natural creative interests.

MY CREATIVE HABIT

We don't believe in adding to your "should-do" list; we want to add to your "can't wait to do" list. Developing an effective creative habit is about finding the right balance between effort and joy. You know the endorphins that kick in after a session at the gym? We want you to feel different after finishing your daily exercise: calmer, more open, and more alive. The benefits of your practice will compound over time if you stick with it.

Take five minutes to set up a dedicated space and time for your daily creative practice. What time of day will work best for you? This will help create a habit that can have a transformative impact on your life.

Where: I will set up a space for my creative practice in

When (time of day):

Notes:

Expert Tip: Pick a consistent time of day and link your daily creative practice to another pleasurable daily habit, such as drinking your coffee in the morning.

YOU'VE INVITED CREATIVITY IN; NOW LET IT INHABIT YOUR (DAILY) LIFE.

THERE ARE INFINITE WAYS TO BE CREATIVE.

HERE ARE A FEW MORE IDEAS FROM US

Create a home altar

Arrange your bookshelf by color
or color combinations

Try flower arranging

Cook with limited ingredients

Try a new instrument

Walk a different way to work

Try a new restaurant

Take photos with your iPhone
and crop to play with scale

Doodle on Zoom calls

Add more color to your outfits

Go vintage shopping

Listen to new music

Go to a music festival

Have an ugly drawing contest with friends

Draw with your nondominant hand
with friends and laugh at the results

Read a book

Learn a new language

Taste new flavors

Sing in the shower

Draw with tape

Garden

HOW ARE YOU CREATIVE?